AF879755

This Instagram Workbook and Planner Belongs to:

If found, contact me here:

Phone: ______________________

Email: ______________________

Address ______________________

Dedicated To

YOU and my clients

Copyright @ 2017 Dwainia Grey

All rights reserved. No part of this book may be reproduced, stored, or transmitted in any form or by any means, including scanning, photocopying, recording, or other electronic or mechanical methods, without the prior written permission of the publisher, except in the case of brief quotations embodied in critical reviews and certain other noncommercial uses permitted by copyright law. For permission requests, email info@awesomebizonline.com subject line "Attention Permissions Coordinator"

Limit of liability/disclaimer of warranty: While the publisher and author have used their best efforts in preparing this workbook and planner, they make no representations or warranties with respect to accuracy or completeness of the contents of this document and specifically disclaim any implied warranties of merchantability or fitness for particular purpose. No warranty may be created or extended by sales representatives, promoters, or written sales materials.

The advice and strategies contained herein may not be suitable for your situation. You should consult with a professional where appropriate. Neither the publisher nor author shall be liable for any loss of profit or any other commercial damages, including but not limited to special, incidental, consequential, or other damages.

Permissions
Please feel free to take photos of this planner (or your use of it) for the purposes of review or social media sharing. Please do not photograph the whole planner.

Published by
GreyChild Communications
Toronto, ON

Instagram Workbook and Planner / Dwainia Grey
ISBN-13: 978-0994888884

ISBN-10: 0994888880

WHAT IS THIS?

This is the **Instagram Workbook and Planner** that will help you succeed with Instagram for your Empowerpreneur business. The book is based on the training in Awesome Nation Engagement; it's a companion book as well as a standalone workbook and planner. The Workbook Section of the book helps you create a Instagram strategy for the year and clarify your Instagram goals and tactics (action steps). The Planner Section of the book helps you plan your monthly Instagram strategy and track your monthly actions and milestones to get a clear picture of your Instagram Return on Investment (ROI).

By having a plan you leverage your time, reach targets (people and goals), add automation and measure success.

HOW TO USE THIS WORKBOOK

The first part is the Strategy Workbook, which includes worksheets and checklists for you to complete. This helps you develop the Instagram Marketing Plan and success strategy for the coming months.

1. Objective	10. Instagram Hashtag Planner
2. Audience	11. Call to Action
3. Style Guide	12. Instagram Photo Planner
4. Engagement in 15 Minutes	13. Instagram Video Planner
5. Do's and Don'ts	14. Instagram Stories Planner
6. Planning	15. Instagram Contest Planner
7. Instagram Post Ideas	16. Getting Started Cheat Sheet
8. 52 Weeks	17. Blog Stats
9. Instagram Profile Worksheet	18. Instagram Yearly Stats

The second section is the **Instagram Action Planner**:

1. Monthly Calendar	6. Instagram Stories Schedule
2. Monthly Success Tracker	7. Instagram Live Tracker
3. Monthly Stats	8. Instagram Campaign Planner
4. Instagram Post Tracker	9. To Do
5. Instagram Video Schedule	10. Notes

The planner section helps you plan your Instagram posts and engagement for the next 12 months. Each month includes monthly planning tools as well as metrics trackers. At the end of each month review the month and start planning for the new month. It's very important to complete your success tracker as it helps you to duplicate success.

The downloadable PDF contains 34 pages and allows you to print pages as needed.

INSTAGRAM TODAY

What is the biggest challenge that you are facing right now with Instagram?

What do you hope to accomplish?

What have you done so far to get your Instagram campaign started?

How much time do you currently spend on Instagram a week?

Are you directing Instagram followers to your email list?

Are you currently using any of the following tools?

- ☐ Instagram
- ☐ Linkedin
- ☐ Twitter
- ☐ YouTube
- ☐ Pinterest
- ☐ Google+
- ☐ Facebook
- ☐ Other sites

Instagram MARKETING

WORKBOOK

Objective

Objective Overall Instagram objective for the year.

- Increase reach
- Build your brand
- Engage influencers and connectors
- Increase customer loyalty
- Drive people to events
- Improve customer service
- Generate leads and sales
- Convert leads to sales

Short-term

Goal # 1 –

Deadline

Action Plan

Goal Met ☐ Yes ☐NO

Goal # 2 –

Deadline

Action Plan

Goal Met ☐ Yes ☐NO

Goal # 3 –

Deadline

Action Plan

Goal Met ☐ Yes ☐NO

Long-term

Goal –

Deadline

Action Plan

Goal Met ☐ Yes ☐NO

Monthly Goal Setter

Set realistic achievable goals for each month.
Goals can be a number of posts or number of new followers to engagement. Make sure it's measurable.

January	February
Goal Met ☐ Yes ☐NO	Goal Met ☐ Yes ☐NO
March	April
Goal Met ☐ Yes ☐NO	Goal Met ☐ Yes ☐NO
May	June
Goal Met ☐ Yes ☐NO	Goal Met ☐ Yes ☐NO
July	August
Goal Met ☐ Yes ☐NO	Goal Met ☐ Yes ☐NO
September	October
Goal Met ☐ Yes ☐NO	Goal Met ☐ Yes ☐NO
November	December
Goal Met ☐ Yes ☐NO	Goal Met ☐ Yes ☐NO

Your Audience

- ☐ Existing clients
- ☐ Prospective clients

Where are they hanging out:

- ☐ Instagram
- ☐ Facebook
- ☐ Twitter
- ☐ Pinterest
- ☐ Google+
- ☐
- ☐
- ☐

Who Are Your Competitors? – How Do They Use Instagram? – How Are You Different?

What Keeps Your Client Up at Night?

How Does Your Product / Service Solve the Problem?

List 3 Successes You Have Had with Clients
Think RESULTS

What Words or Phrases Do Your Clients Use to Describe the Problem?	What Words or Phrases Do Your Clients Use When They are Looking for the Solution? (KEYWORDS)

Your Avatar

Name (fictitious):
Gender:
Age:
Profession:
Marital and Family Status:
Associations:
Location (city, neighborhood, or postal code):

Style Guide

Instagram MARKETING

Image Text 1

Font
Size
Style
Color
Hex
RGB
CMYK

Image Text 2

Font
Size
Style
Color
Hex
RGB
CMYK

Watermark Text 1

Font
Size
Style
Color
Hex
RGB
CMYK

Image Sizes

Profile 110 x 110 px

Post Template 1080 x 1080 px

Show placement of graphics, watermark, text alignment, borders etc.

Notes

Separate post templates for blog posts, quotes, promotions, etc?

Create templates using Photoshop, Canva or Picmonkey.

Voice, tone, abbreviations, spellings, and punctuation to use:

Filters, frames, shape: square, portrait, and landscape images (resize images for consistency):

15 Minutes A Day of Engagement

	Day 1	Day 2
3-5 Minutes	**Like, and comment on other people's content as well as your clients.**	**Like and comment on other people's content. as well as your clients.**
1-5 Minutes	**Notifications** ☐ Answer Comments (Good and Bad) ☐ Respond, ask more questions, and provide support	**Notifications** ☐ Answer Comments (Good and Bad) ☐ Respond, ask more questions, and provide support
1-5 Minutes	**Connect with Brands** ☐ Like, comment, and @Tag them when using their products.	**Make A New Friend** ☐ Influencers and Brands ☐ Current, Past and Future Clients ☐ Future Collaborators

POST A PHOTO DAILY

Increase Engagement by Integrating Instagram on Your Website

- ☐ Instagram Profile buttons
- ☐ Instagram Widget
- ☐ Embed Instagram posts on blog posts

Make a Connection

- ☐ Choose someone you want to connect with
- ☐ Like and comment on 1 photo everyday

Instagram Do's and Don'ts

Instagram MARKETING

- ☐ Always follow the rules and regulations for Instagram.
- ☐ Do create a social media marketing plan, but adjust your specific tactics as you go. Be flexible and take the time to find out what works and what doesn't work.
- ☐ Do pay attention to social media ethics.
- ☐ Don't be disrespectful, offensive, vulgar or use language considered to be inflammatory. Don't be rude or difficult to deal with when engaging with your followers.
- ☐ Do make your account public.
- ☐ Do connect to Facebook.
- ☐ Do use call to action buttons.
- ☐ Do use an URL shortener such as bitly.
- ☐ Do use Instagram Ads.
- ☐ Don't lie to your audience or hide the fact that you are advertising to them. Always be transparent with your intentions.
- ☐ Do commit the time and effort to maintain your Instagram marketing plan.
- ☐ Do prepare to deal with how online users change, alter, or use your brand's message. Have a plan for both good and bad customer feedback.
- ☐ Do interact with people by liking and commenting on their posts.
- ☐ Do engage with people who have similar interests.
- ☐ Do engage with followers content.
- ☐ Do support the promotional campaigns of other non-competitive businesses and your followers.
- ☐ Do answer all messages and mentions in a timely manner.
- ☐ Do respond promptly to all comments.
- ☐ Do repost other people's content.
- ☐ Do respond to non-spammy mentions.
- ☐ Do mention people and brands where appropriate using the @tag.
- ☐ Do encourage people to post using your products and the right custom branded hashtag.
- ☐ Do get permission before using photos of clients using your products.
- ☐ Do create a call to action in each post and refer people to your link in profile to drive traffic to your website.
- ☐ Don't overdo it when promoting your business. You want to use Instagram to build relationships not overwhelm people with promotions.
- ☐ Do use images to entertain and inspire.
- ☐ Do post consistently and frequently.

Instagram Do's and Don'ts

Instagram MARKETING

- ☐ Do post videos, and stories.
- ☐ Don't just post your own content.
- ☐ Do provide information on post captions and use relevant hashtags.
- ☐ Don't overuse exclamations, quotation marks, emojis, and icons.
- ☐ Do test captions long vs. short.
- ☐ Do use style sheets, templates, and the same filters for brand consistency.
- ☐ Do use relevant captions and hashtags.
- ☐ Don't overuse hashtags.
- ☐ Do use geo-tagging where applicable. Increases engagement and SEO.
- ☐ Do tag brands and influencers in your photos.
- ☐ Do use tagging properly. Only tag people you know or brands when using their products, wearing their apparel, or promoting their work.
- ☐ Don't tag people you don't know on your posts unless you are promoting them.
- ☐ Don't post more than 5 images per an hour or too many images at once – it is considered spam.
- ☐ Don't spam!
- ☐ Do Batch It: Prepare multiple branded images for posts, blog posts to share daily.
- ☐ Do follow hashtags.
- ☐ Do follow associations and groups.
- ☐ Don't forget to add attribution when it's not your content. Use the @ tag.
- ☐ Do pay attention to the metrics and analytics of your campaign.
- ☐ Do find the perfect time to post.
- ☐ Do reward loyal followers who engage with you on a regular basis with products, samples, reports, or Skype or phone call consultation (DO NOT ASK FOR SALE).
- ☐ Do send people to an opt-in page to capture and track emails.
- ☐ **Do Use Instagram Search**
    - ☐ On a regular basis, use search to find potential clients and people to follow by using key phrases (and words).
    - ☐ Follow new people, and hashtags of current and potential clients.
    - ☐ Search misspellings of your Instagram handle, your name, and business - Monitor your brands hashtags.
    - ☐ Search using relevant and complementary hashtags.

Day-to-Day Management

How many times a week will you post on Instagram?
Suggested number of times a week to post: max 3 daily

What days and times will you post?

How far ahead do you want to plan content?

How often will you promote your own content (blog posts, events, products and services) versus other people's content?

What type of content are you going to share? Review the Post Idea Sheet. What you share needs to bring value - always think "What's in it for me?" Try for a combination of educating, and engaging. You are aiming to get them interested in you, your brand, and your business.

Who will create content? Images / Video / Copy

Who will post content?

Who will manage your Instagram campaigns?

Who will track, monitor, and report?

Number of people to follow each week:

Do you want to assign posts to certain days a week? Throwback Thursday, Follow Friday, or make up your own

	Themed Post	Create Content	Publish Content
Monday			
Tuesday			
Wednesday			
Thursday			
Friday			
Saturday			
Sunday			

Resources

- ☐ Experienced Writer
- ☐ Professional Photos / Photo shoot
- ☐ Professional Videos / Video shoot
- ☐ Branded Graphics

Instagram Policy

Develop your Instagram Policy.
Read the Do's and Don'ts of Instagram. What are the policies you will have for your Empowerpreneur business?

- Rules of engagement
- How to handle customer service
- What to say and what not to say
- Workflow / Schedule
- How to handle negative feedback /criticism
    - Clients, media or competitors

Budget

Startup and launch budget
Campaign budgets
Ongoing management budget
- Advertising
- Design Tools (Canva, Pic Monkey, Hootsuite, Buffer, etc)

Metrics

Review your online metrics on a weekly and/or monthly basis. Use Iconosquare in conjunction with bitly, to track and monitor your success.

Learn more about your return on investment (ROI – time and money) as well as which posts brings the most traffic, engagement and conversion.

Take time to complete the Blog Stats, Monthly Success Tracker, and The Monthly and Yearly Social Media Stats.

Va Va VooM ™

Va Va VooM ™ (Content Marketing Ratio)

Value – 40% - Tips, tutorials, and instructional useful and helpful posts

List 3 topics that you can post about that will add value

Visual – 20% - Make use of videos (Post up to 60 second videos on Instagram)

List 3 ways you can use videos on Instagram

Voice – 30% - Show your personality – personal posts about you, showing your life, and a behind the scenes view

List 3 posts that will show your personality

Marketing – 10% - Promotional posts to sell and promote your products and services

List 3 products / services you want to sell / promote via social media

Content Ideas for Instagram

1	**Valuable and Useful Information, Tips and Ideas,**	2	**Blog Posts** Ensure every blog has a branded image sized for Instagram.	3	**Influencer's Posts** Tag and repost influencers and brand accounts	4	**Personal Posts** - Updates - Behind-the-scenes - Scenery - Lifestyle
5	**Before and After**	6	**Weekly Series or Q & A**	7	**Instagram Exclusives**	8	**Events, Workshops and Seminars** Share online and offline events you are hosting or attending
9	**Your Work** Post updates about your work, and images from your portfolio.	10	**Meaningful moments / emotional / funny posts / food**	11	**Testimonials** Show happy clients using your products and services. Quote testimonials.	12	**Business News** Updates about your business and industry.
13	**Quotes** Post quotes that will motivate and inspire your audience.	14	**Products / Services** - Showcase your products and services - Pre-release to build buzz - Sales	15	**60 Second Videos & Stories** Showcase your product, product demos, updates, commercials, teasers, tutorials, testimonials, and trailers.	16	**Launch and Pre-Launch** Build momentum with images, photos, videos, and Instagram Live.
17	**Promotions** Promote your products, services, sales, flash sales, coupons and launches, etc.	18	**Contests and Giveaways** Use contests, giveaways, and sweepstakes	19	**Repost** Repost images of your products used by others on Instagram and other Social Media platforms..	20	**Celebrate Milestones / Anniversaries** Have a sale or giveaway for reaching 1,000 followers

52 Weeks

Instagram MARKETING

Plan out 52 weeks of Tips, Quotes, etc
52 Weeks of ___________________________

1		27	
2		28	
3		29	
4		30	
5		31	
6		32	
7		33	
8		34	
9		35	
10		36	
11		37	
12		38	
13		39	
14		40	
15		41	
16		42	
17		43	
18		44	
19		45	
20		46	
21		47	
22		48	
23		49	
24		50	
25		51	
26		52	

Instagram Profile

- ☐ Professional profile image, logo, logo mark (no words), mascot or product
- ☐ Name and Username – Use your real name and/or company name
- ☐ Bio – Branded, search optimized profile (150 characters)
  - Stand out with line breaks, emojis, branded hashtags, list of other accounts
- ☐ Website URL (landing page, shop page or link relevant to latest post)
- ☐ Category (ensure your Facebook Page Category is optimized)
- ☐ Call to Action Button (only visible in app view)
  - Call (phone number)
  - Email (professional email address)
  - Directions (add address if you have a physical location)

Optimized Bio

Hashtags

Using Hashtags

- ☐ Always include Hashtags so it's easy to find you.
- ☐ Only use relevant hashtags.
- ☐ The goal is to be included in the top 9 popular posts on Explore with most engagement.
- ☐ Brainstorm keywords and trends. (Use the hashtag worksheet). Use a mix of hashtags:
  - ☐ Brand Hashtag (business name, slogan, products and services)
  - ☐ Campaign Hashtag (unique marketing campaign hashtag)
  - ☐ General Hashtag appeals to larger audience (generic hashtag relevant to your business (you are a coach: #coach)
  - ☐ Industry Hashtag
  - ☐ Trending Hashtag (relevant to your brand and post)
- ☐ Include hashtags at the bottom of caption or in the first comment.

Custom / Brand Hashtags

Industry Hashtags

Hashtags

#Hashtags to Use	✓

Use hashtags. List popular hashtags for your preferred client, industry, and niche (as well as lifestyle, event, and location). Create branded hashtags for your business, campaigns, and products and services. Remember to use trending hashtags. Use only relevant hashtags.

Call To Action

At least once a week, tell your followers what you want them to do by using a Call To Action. A Call To Action can be “link in profile”, “tag your friends”, “share this”, “repost”, "register", "download", “double tap if you agree”, or “like this”. Make it short, concise and easy to action.

Call To Action	✓

Photo Planner

Instagram MARKETING

Photo Tips

- ☐ Ensure your photos align with your objective, theme and brand. Plan ahead. Tell your story.
- ☐ Get to know your phone camera, your photo apps and filters.
- ☐ Think quality over quantity while posting consistently and frequently.
- ☐ Take multiple shots and choose the best.

Taking Photos

- ☐ Focus - Have a focal point, a clear point of interest by make each photo have a single subject (don't clutter)
- ☐ Background - use textures, patterns, color and movement.
- ☐ Use natural light as much as possible - take photos near a window, away from artificial light. You can use sunrise or sunset for contrast.
- ☐ Don't be afraid of bad weather and cloudy days. Can add distinction to your images.
- ☐ Don't use flash. Avoid if possible.
- ☐ Don't zoom. Images may come out grainy, blurry or pixelated. You can get closer and crop later.
- ☐ Composition
  - ☐ Use the rule of thirds for balance. Turn on the grid feature on your camera phone.
  - ☐ Use different perspectives - take photos from the top or different angles.
  - ☐ Use Negative Space (white space) - the empty space around the subject effectively
  - ☐ Background and foreground - pay attention to what's in the picture (dirty dishes not cool)
  - ☐ Don't be afraid of props.
  - ☐ Don't be afraid of candid shots.
- ☐ Photo Types:
  - ☐ Nature - great for travel blogs
  - ☐ People - always ask permission
  - ☐ Perfect Wall Background - great for fashion
  - ☐ Scenic - Landscape and cityscape
  - ☐ Top Down / Flat Lay - great for food
  - ☐ Travel - can include nature, people, and scenic photos
  - ☐
  - ☐

Editing

- ☐ Photos can be
  - ☐ Square (1080 px x 1080 px)
  - ☐ Landscape (1080 px x 566 px)
  - ☐ Portrait (1080 x 1350 px).
- ☐ Always crop the same way. I recommend cropping to square for consistency and when you look at your profile page all the images are shown as square.
- ☐ Add filters (use the same filters for consistency)
- ☐ Don't over edit - keep it simple. Use Photoshop, VSCO, Snapseed or any good photo editing software or app.
- ☐ Have fun!

Photo Planner

Instagram MARKETING

Photo Ideas

Tips

- ☐ Use relevant caption (max length 2,500 characters)
- ☐ Make the first 3-4 lines of the caption count as they are visible
- ☐ Always include a Call to Action: Ask for comments, ask a question, fill in the blanks, or caption this, etc.
- ☐ Tag customers, influencers and brands
- ☐ Geo tag where applicable
- ☐ Always include Hashtags
- ☐ Use the carousel feature and add up to 10 images and video.

List Call To Actions

List Hashtags

Video Planner

Instagram MARKETING

A Minute of Video is Worth 1.8 Million Words - Dr. James McQuivey

Video Tips

Videos help build trust and help develop relationships. After watching a video, followers are more likely to buy.

- ☐ 3 - 60 Seconds
- ☐ Use videos to tell your story and convey your marketing message.
- ☐ Use brand colors, themes and imagery
- ☐ Videos are great for:
    - ☐ Behind the Scenes
    - ☐ DIY (Do-It-Yourself)
    - ☐ Highlight products
    - ☐ Product launch
    - ☐ Short commercials
    - ☐ Show emotion
    - ☐ Show happy customers and you interacting with them
    - ☐ Show the process - how its made
    - ☐ Showcase your work like a portfolio
    - ☐ Showcase special offers
    - ☐ Video Tutorials
- ☐ Make videos as beautiful as a photo to quickly capture attention (first 3-5 seconds) and convey your message.
- ☐ You can post videos with or without sound and auto-play in the feed, but they don't start playing sound automatically. Remember video starts without sound, so delay audio.
- ☐ Get your point across without audio. Design for sound off. Use text overlay and subtitles and your logo.
- ☐ User vertical videos for stories and horizontal for your news feed
- ☐ Edit with professional software or mobile apps

Video Planner

Instagram MARKETING

Video Ideas

Tips

- ☐ Create a brief, intriguing caption to entice followers to watch
- ☐ Use relevant and descriptive hashtags
- ☐ Use Boomerang to loop the video
- ☐ Use Hyperlapse to condense videos with a playback speed 1x to12x
- ☐ You can also share videos in direct messages (DM)

List Call To Actions

List Hashtags

Stories Planner

Instagram MARKETING

Tell Your Stories

Stories are a great way to share and promote your content. The aim with Instagram Stories and going live is to end up on the explore page, where millions of people can find you. Stories allow you to post more frequently and not overload your feed.

- ☐ Ensure that your stories are made public in the Instagram settings.
- ☐ 10 second story that disappears in 24 hours unless you pin it
- ☐ Photo or video
- ☐ Optimal Size: 750 px x 1334 px
- ☐ Tag relevant people and businesses.
- ☐ Include a call to action
- ☐ **Use Stories Highlights** - You can pin any story you have shared in the past to your profile. It will stay on your profile page until you remove and can only be seen on your profile page when someone visits.
- ☐ **Use Stores Archive** - You can save all your stories to the archive and share when you want in the Stories Highlights. Your archives are only visible to you.

Instagram Stories Ideas

- ☐ Announcements
- ☐ Behind the scenes #bts
- ☐ Poll
- ☐ Press and Press mentions
- ☐ Host an Instagram takeover (someone else can host your account from their perspective) Great way to brand and cross promote.
- ☐ Rants

Go Live

Instagram Live - Real Time

You can use the stories function and go live. Instagram Live allows you to expand your reach and gain extra visibility. Instagram Live is great for engagement; followers can interact with comments and likes. Gain your followers attention as they are notified when you go live.

- ☐ For each story or live post, have an objective.
- ☐ Have a script ready or talking points.
- ☐ Practice by recording yourself first.
- ☐ You don't have to be perfect.
- ☐ Optimal size 1080 px X 920 px
- ☐ Save your live post to your stories, so it can live for 24 hours.
- ☐ You can share on other social media platforms by saving it.
- ☐ Promote your live in advance in the days and hours leading up to your broadcast. Promote on other social media platforms too. Let people know when you will be going live (don't forget time zone).

Instagram Live Ideas

- ☐ Announcements
- ☐ Behind the scenes
- ☐ Demos
- ☐ Lessons and tutorials
- ☐ New products - tease, pre-launch and launch
- ☐ Q & A's
- ☐ Takeovers
- ☐ Promotions:
  - ☐ Contests
    - ☐ Discounts (share coupon codes)
    - ☐ Flash sales
    - ☐ Giveaways

Stories Planner

Instagram MARKETING

Story Ideas

Notes

Live Ideas

Contest Planner

Instagram MARKETING

Contests are an effective way to build engagement, get more followers and grow your brand. Use contests to promote your business and expand brand awareness.

Contest Checklist

- ☐ Follow Instagram Promotion Guidelines.
- ☐ What's your contest theme and objective?
- ☐ Create contest terms and conditions. Include:
  - ☐ Rules
  - ☐ Contest deadline (clear start and end date)
  - ☐ Eligibility
  - ☐ Requirements for entry
  - ☐ Restrictions
  - ☐ When you will announce the winner
- ☐ Ask them to follow you as a condition.
- ☐ Provide an awesome relevant prize. The prize should also be an incentive to share the post.
- ☐ Create multiple images to promote your contest. Use graphics, photos and video.
- ☐ Make it easy to enter. Don't have multiple ways to enter.

Promote

- ☐ Create a branded contest hashtag. Contest hashtags should be short, relevant, memorable and unique. Don't' forget to include #contest and #giveaway
- ☐ Promote contest on your profile.
- ☐ Promote contest on your blog and other social media platforms as well as your mailing list.

Manage

- ☐ Manage your contest. Engage with participants and offer encouragement.
- ☐ Analyze the contest.
  - ☐ Number of participants and submissions.
  - ☐ Engagement
  - ☐ Follower's growth.
  - ☐ Website traffic
  - ☐ Sales

Follow Up

- ☐ Announce the winner with an image.
- ☐ Thank the other participants directly via a post or email.

Have Fun!

Choose your type of contest:

- ☐ Like to Win Contest - like post to qualify.
- ☐ Comment to Win Contest - comment on post to qualify. You can reward best comment.
- ☐ Caption Contest - caption the image to qualify. You can reward the best caption.
- ☐ Hashtag Contest - Get followers to post images and use the branded campaign hashtag.
- ☐ Photo / Selfie Contest - follower must post a photo using the product or taking the action you specify using the branded campaign hashtag. This is a great promotion to use across social media platforms.
- ☐ Repost Contest - repost the image to qualify and use the branded campaign hashtag and/or tag.
- ☐ Tag Contest - tag a friend in the comments section to qualify. User can also tag their friend (nominate) to win the contest or they can both win.
- ☐ Tag a Photo Contest - tag someone or post a new photo and tag someone.
- ☐ User Generated Contest - Ask users to post a photo or video with the branded campaign hashtag.
- ☐ Complicated Contest - doing a combination or all of the above to qualify.
- ☐ Loop Contest - this is a great way to cross promote others by getting followers to take action on the accounts of all prize givers to qualify.
- ☐ Consider an Instagram Contest Promotion App.

Contest Planner

Instagram MARKETING

Contest Ideas

Contest Themes

Contest Hashtags

*Use the Campaign Manager to plan your next contest.

NOTES

Getting Started Cheat Sheet

Instagram MARKETING

Branding

- ☐ I have a clear description of who my target audience is.
- ☐ My preferred client is using Instagram.
- ☐ I have included a professional photo or logo on my Instagram profile.
- ☐ My Instagram name is easy to find, follow, and connect with.
  - ☐ It's my name, business name, brand name, or based on an SEO keyword.
  - ☐ It's the same as my other social media profile names for consistency
- ☐ I have a completed Instagram profile.
- ☐ Bio section reflects my voice and brand and includes keywords and website URL.
- ☐ I know what personality/ brand message and image I want to communicate.
- ☐ I have included my business location (where applicable - at least put country).
- ☐ I have created an Instagram Business Account.
  - ☐ I have an optimized Business Facebook Page
  - ☐ I have included contact information for Call to Action Buttons (Phone, Email, Address - where applicable)

Planning

- ☐ I know my Instagram objective.
- ☐ I have defined my Instagram marketing goals and know how I will track them.
- ☐ I've created systems to test and track my social media marketing goals and tactics.
- ☐ I have a *Social Media Marketing Plan* that I use to help guide my online marketing and I've integrated my Instagram marketing tactics into my overall social media marketing strategies.
- ☐ I've use automation tools such as Iconsquare to optimize my time.
- ☐ I've documented the systems and tools I use, so it can be easily delegated.
- ☐ I use Instagram Insights to create targeted posts and know the best day and time for engagement.
- ☐ I use Instagram Advertising.
- ☐ I have a (monthly/ weekly / daily) posting schedule for Instagram.
- ☐ I have a (monthly/ weekly/ daily) Instagram engagement schedule.
  - ☐ Post Updates
  - ☐ Respond to all messages and comments
  - ☐ Mention people when you post their content or products
  - ☐ Connect with brands
- ☐ I have a strategy to capture leads from Instagram and to get followers to buy.

Getting Started Cheat Sheet

Instagram **MARKETING**

Content

- ☐ I have developed a system to find valuable content to share on Instagram.
- ☐ I make sure I share a good mix of content (*Va Va VooM* – Value, Voice, Visual and Marketing).
- ☐ I use a Call To Action in posts.
- ☐ I'm creating specific promotions and offers for my Instagram audience – *EXCLUSIVE.*
- ☐ I use an editorial calendar to layout content for my blog, and Instagram posts.
- ☐ I schedule blog posts as they are published.
- ☐ I allow followers to see and reply to my Instagram Stories.
- ☐ I use Instagram Insights to find the optimal day and time to post content for maximum engagement.
- ☐ I follow the top bloggers in my industry to stay on top of trends.
- ☐ I create specific content to share on Instagram.
- ☐ I always check for grammar and spelling.

Instagram Tools

- ☐ A Beatiful Mess
- ☐ AutoGrammer
- ☐ Buffer
- ☐ Canva
- ☐ Hootsuite
- ☐ Hyperlapse
- ☐ Iconosquare
- ☐ Latergram
- ☐ Layout
- ☐ Photo Grid
- ☐ Picmonkey
- ☐ PicsArt
- ☐ Pixlr
- ☐ Schedugram
- ☐ Snapseed
- ☐ VSCO

Blog Stats

	Date	Instagram	Facebook	Google+	Pinterest	Twitter	Blog Visits
1							
2							
3							
4							
5							
6							
7							
8							
9							
10							
11							
12							
13							
14							
15							
16							
17							
18							
19							
20							
21							
22							
23							
24							
25							
26							
27							
28							
29							
30							
31							
32							
33							
34							
35							
36							
37							
38							
39							
40							
41							
42							
43							
44							
45							
46							
47							
48							
49							
50							
51							
52							

Yearly Stats

Year	Total Followers		# of Reposts		# of Posts		# of Likes		# of Comments		# of Clicks to Website	
	Goal	Actual	Goal	Actual	Goal	Actual	Goal	Actual	Goal	Actual	Goal	Actual
January												
February												
March												
April												
May												
June												
July												
August												
September												
October												
November												
December												
Yearly Total												

Instagram
MARKETING
PLANNER

Month

SUNDAY	MONDAY	TUESDAY	WEDNESDAY	THURSDAY	FRIDAY	SATURDAY

Notes

Acknowledge and Celebrate Your Success

Month:

Total Followers

Post with most engagement (Reposts, Likes, and Comments) on Instagram

---

Post with most clicks

Blog post with most traffic from Instagram

This month, I learned

A record I broke this month

My celebration this month

Next month, I plan to do the same

Next month, I plan to try (new)

Monthly Stats

GOAL:

Total Followers	New Followers	# of Posts	# of Reposts	# of Likes	# of Comments	# of Mentions	# of Clicks	# of Clicks to Website

EMAIL SUBSCRIBERS FROM INSTAGRAM	

ENGAGEMENT

Post with most reposts	
Post with most likes	
Post with most comments	
Post with most clicks	

INSTAGRAM ADS

Spend $		Results	

Post Tracker

Instagram Posts	Call to Action	Date	Time	✓

Post Tracker

Instagram Posts	Call to Action	Date	Time	✓

Video Schedule

Video	Date	Time	✓
#			
#			
#			
#			
#			
#			
#			
#			
#			
#			
#			
#			
#			
#			
#			
#			
#			
#			
#			
#			
#			
#			
#			
#			
#			
#			
#			

Stories Schedule

Instagram MARKETING

Use Instagram stories to boost engagement. Post photos in a slideshow or a quick video that will be gone in 24 hours. Perfect for announcements, rants and behind-the-scenes posts.

Stories	Date	Time	✓
#			
#			
#			
#			
#			
#			
#			
#			
#			
#			
#			
#			
#			
#			
#			
#			
#			
#			
#			
#			
#			
#			
#			
#			
#			
#			

Live Tracker

Instagram Live	Date	Time	✓
#			
#			
#			
#			
#			
#			
#			
#			
#			
#			
#			
#			
#			
#			
#			
#			
#			
#			
#			
#			
#			
#			
#			
#			
#			
#			

Product / Service Campaign

Campaign	
Description	
Product / Service / Newsletter / Contest / Giveaway	
Start	End
Objective	
Target Audience	
Budget$ / Cost$ / Return$	
Landing Page	
Tracking Link	
Days and Time	
Winner / Date Notified	

Image

- ☐ Blog Post Announcement
- ☐ Blog Post Follow-up
- ☐ Autoresponder Setup
- ☐ Ad Campaign
  - Budget$
  - Cost$
  - Return$
  - Click Thru Rate
  - CPC (Cost per Click)
- ☐ Conversion Rate
- ☐ Hashtag
- ☐ Coupon Code (if applicable)

Advertising Campaign

Campaign	
Boost / Ad	
Description	
Start	End
Objective	
Target Audience	
Budget$ / Cost Per Day$	
Landing Page	
Tracking Link	

Text

Demographic

Image

To Do

	Priority	Completed

Notes

Month

SUNDAY	MONDAY	TUESDAY	WEDNESDAY	THURSDAY	FRIDAY	SATURDAY

Notes

Acknowledge and Celebrate Your Success

Month:

Total Followers

Post with most engagement (Reposts, Likes, and Comments) on Instagram

---

Post with most clicks

Blog post with most traffic from Instagram

This month, I learned

A record I broke this month

My celebration this month

Next month, I plan to do the same

Next month, I plan to try (new)

Monthly Stats

GOAL:

Total Followers	New Followers	# of Posts	# of Reposts	# of Likes	# of Comments	# of Mentions	# of Clicks	# of Clicks to Website

EMAIL SUBSCRIBERS FROM INSTAGRAM	
ENGAGEMENT	
Post with most reposts	
Post with most likes	
Post with most comments	
Post with most clicks	
INSTAGRAM ADS	

Spend $		Results	

Post Tracker

Instagram Posts	Call to Action	Date	Time	✓

Post Tracker

Instagram MARKETING

Instagram Posts	Call to Action	Date	Time	✓

Video Schedule

Video	Date	Time	✓
#			
#			
#			
#			
#			
#			
#			
#			
#			
#			
#			
#			
#			
#			
#			
#			
#			
#			
#			
#			
#			
#			
#			
#			
#			
#			
#			

Stories Schedule

Instagram MARKETING

Use Instagram stories to boost engagement. Post photos in a slideshow or a quick video that will be gone in 24 hours. Perfect for announcements, rants and behind-the-scenes posts.

Stories	Date	Time	✓
#			
#			
#			
#			
#			
#			
#			
#			
#			
#			
#			
#			
#			
#			
#			
#			
#			
#			
#			
#			
#			
#			
#			
#			
#			
#			

Live Tracker

Instagram MARKETING

Instagram Live	Date	Time	✓
#			
#			
#			
#			
#			
#			
#			
#			
#			
#			
#			
#			
#			
#			
#			
#			
#			
#			
#			
#			
#			
#			
#			
#			
#			
#			

Product / Service Campaign

Campaign	
Description	
Product / Service / Newsletter / Contest / Giveaway	
Start	End
Objective	
Target Audience	
Budget$ / Cost$ / Return$	
Landing Page	
Tracking Link	
Days and Time	
Winner / Date Notified	

Image

- ☐ Blog Post Announcement
- ☐ Blog Post Follow-up
- ☐ Autoresponder Setup
- ☐ Ad Campaign
  - Budget$
  - Cost$
  - Return$
  - Click Thru Rate
  - CPC (Cost per Click)
- ☐ Conversion Rate
- ☐ Hashtag
- ☐ Coupon Code (if applicable)

Advertising Campaign

Campaign	
Boost / Ad	
Description	
Start	End
Objective	
Target Audience	
Budget$ / Cost Per Day$	
Landing Page	
Tracking Link	

Text	Demographic

Image

To Do

	Priority	Completed

Month

SUNDAY	MONDAY	TUESDAY	WEDNESDAY	THURSDAY	FRIDAY	SATURDAY

Notes

Acknowledge and Celebrate Your Success

Month:

Total Followers

Post with most engagement (Reposts, Likes, and Comments) on Instagram

Post with most clicks

Blog post with most traffic from Instagram

This month, I learned

A record I broke this month

My celebration this month

Next month, I plan to do the same

Next month, I plan to try (new)

Monthly Stats

GOAL:

Total Followers	New Followers	# of Posts	# of Reposts	# of Likes	# of Comments	# of Mentions	# of Clicks	# of Clicks to Website

EMAIL SUBSCRIBERS FROM INSTAGRAM	
ENGAGEMENT	
Post with most reposts	
Post with most likes	
Post with most comments	
Post with most clicks	
INSTAGRAM ADS	

Spend $		Results	

Post Tracker

Instagram Posts	Call to Action	Date	Time	✓

Post Tracker

Instagram Posts	Call to Action	Date	Time	✓

Video Schedule

Instagram MARKETING

Video	Date	Time	✓
#			
#			
#			
#			
#			
#			
#			
#			
#			
#			
#			
#			
#			
#			
#			
#			
#			
#			
#			
#			
#			
#			
#			
#			
#			
#			
#			

Stories Schedule

Instagram MARKETING

Use Instagram stories to boost engagement. Post photos in a slideshow or a quick video that will be gone in 24 hours. Perfect for announcements, rants and behind-the-scenes posts.

Stories	Date	Time	✓
#			
#			
#			
#			
#			
#			
#			
#			
#			
#			
#			
#			
#			
#			
#			
#			
#			
#			
#			
#			
#			
#			
#			
#			
#			
#			

Live Tracker

Instagram Live	Date	Time	✓
#			
#			
#			
#			
#			
#			
#			
#			
#			
#			
#			
#			
#			
#			
#			
#			
#			
#			
#			
#			
#			
#			
#			
#			
#			
#			

Product / Service Campaign

Campaign	
Description	
Product / Service / Newsletter / Contest / Giveaway	
Start	End
Objective	
Target Audience	
Budget$ / Cost$ / Return$	
Landing Page	
Tracking Link	
Days and Time	
Winner / Date Notified	

Image

- ☐ Blog Post Announcement
- ☐ Blog Post Follow-up
- ☐ Autoresponder Setup
- ☐ Ad Campaign
  - Budget$
  - Cost$
  - Return$
  - Click Thru Rate
  - CPC (Cost per Click)
- ☐ Conversion Rate
- ☐ Hashtag
- ☐ Coupon Code (if applicable)

Advertising Campaign

Campaign	
Boost / Ad	
Description	
Start	End
Objective	
Target Audience	
Budget$ / Cost Per Day$	
Landing Page	
Tracking Link	

Text

Demographic

Image

To Do

	Priority	Completed

Month

SUNDAY	MONDAY	TUESDAY	WEDNESDAY	THURSDAY	FRIDAY	SATURDAY

Notes

Acknowledge and Celebrate Your Success

Month:

Total Followers

Post with most engagement (Reposts, Likes, and Comments) on Instagram

---

Post with most clicks

Blog post with most traffic from Instagram

This month, I learned

A record I broke this month

My celebration this month

Next month, I plan to do the same

Next month, I plan to try (new)

Monthly Stats

GOAL:

Total Followers	New Followers	# of Posts	# of Reposts	# of Likes	# of Comments	# of Mentions	# of Clicks	# of Clicks to Website

EMAIL SUBSCRIBERS FROM INSTAGRAM	
ENGAGEMENT	
Post with most reposts	
Post with most likes	
Post with most comments	
Post with most clicks	
INSTAGRAM ADS	

Spend $		Results	

Post Tracker

Instagram Posts	Call to Action	Date	Time	✓

Post Tracker

Instagram Posts	Call to Action	Date	Time	✓

Video Schedule

Video	Date	Time	✓
#			
#			
#			
#			
#			
#			
#			
#			
#			
#			
#			
#			
#			
#			
#			
#			
#			
#			
#			
#			
#			
#			
#			
#			
#			
#			
#			

Stories Schedule

Instagram MARKETING

Use Instagram stories to boost engagement. Post photos in a slideshow or a quick video that will be gone in 24 hours. Perfect for announcements, rants and behind-the-scenes posts.

Stories	Date	Time	✓
#			
#			
#			
#			
#			
#			
#			
#			
#			
#			
#			
#			
#			
#			
#			
#			
#			
#			
#			
#			
#			
#			
#			
#			
#			
#			

Live Tracker

Instagram Live	Date	Time	✓
#			
#			
#			
#			
#			
#			
#			
#			
#			
#			
#			
#			
#			
#			
#			
#			
#			
#			
#			
#			
#			
#			
#			
#			
#			
#			

Product / Service Campaign

Campaign	
Description	
Product / Service / Newsletter / Contest / Giveaway	
Start	End
Objective	
Target Audience	
Budget$ / Cost$ / Return$	
Landing Page	
Tracking Link	
Days and Time	
Winner / Date Notified	

Image

- ☐ Blog Post Announcement
- ☐ Blog Post Follow-up
- ☐ Autoresponder Setup
- ☐ Ad Campaign
  - Budget$
  - Cost$
  - Return$
  - Click Thru Rate
  - CPC (Cost per Click)
- ☐ Conversion Rate
- ☐ Hashtag
- ☐ Coupon Code (if applicable)

Advertising Campaign

Campaign	
Boost / Ad	
Description	
Start	End
Objective	
Target Audience	
Budget$ / Cost Per Day$	
Landing Page	
Tracking Link	

Text

Demographic

Image

To Do

	Priority	Completed

Month

SUNDAY	MONDAY	TUESDAY	WEDNESDAY	THURSDAY	FRIDAY	SATURDAY

Notes

Acknowledge and Celebrate Your Success

Month:

Total Followers

Post with most engagement (Reposts, Likes, and Comments) on Instagram

---

Post with most clicks

Blog post with most traffic from Instagram

This month, I learned

A record I broke this month

My celebration this month

Next month, I plan to do the same

Next month, I plan to try (new)

Monthly Stats

GOAL:

Total Followers	New Followers	# of Posts	# of Reposts	# of Likes	# of Comments	# of Mentions	# of Clicks	# of Clicks to Website

EMAIL SUBSCRIBERS FROM INSTAGRAM	
ENGAGEMENT	
Post with most reposts	
Post with most likes	
Post with most comments	
Post with most clicks	
INSTAGRAM ADS	

Spend $		Results	

Post Tracker

Instagram Posts	Call to Action	Date	Time	✓

Post Tracker

Instagram Posts	Call to Action	Date	Time	✓

Video Schedule

Video	Date	Time	✓
#			
#			
#			
#			
#			
#			
#			
#			
#			
#			
#			
#			
#			
#			
#			
#			
#			
#			
#			
#			
#			
#			
#			
#			
#			
#			
#			

Stories Schedule

Use Instagram stories to boost engagement. Post photos in a slideshow or a quick video that will be gone in 24 hours. Perfect for announcements, rants and behind-the-scenes posts.

Stories	Date	Time	✓
#			
#			
#			
#			
#			
#			
#			
#			
#			
#			
#			
#			
#			
#			
#			
#			
#			
#			
#			
#			
#			
#			
#			
#			
#			
#			

Live Tracker

Instagram Live	Date	Time	✓
#			
#			
#			
#			
#			
#			
#			
#			
#			
#			
#			
#			
#			
#			
#			
#			
#			
#			
#			
#			
#			
#			
#			
#			
#			
#			

Product / Service Campaign

Campaign	
Description	
Product / Service / Newsletter / Contest / Giveaway	
Start	End
Objective	
Target Audience	
Budget$ / Cost$ / Return$	
Landing Page	
Tracking Link	
Days and Time	
Winner / Date Notified	

Image

- ☐ Blog Post Announcement
- ☐ Blog Post Follow-up
- ☐ Autoresponder Setup
- ☐ Ad Campaign
  - Budget$
  - Cost$
  - Return$
  - Click Thru Rate
  - CPC (Cost per Click)
- ☐ Conversion Rate
- ☐ Hashtag
- ☐ Coupon Code (if applicable)

Advertising Campaign

Campaign	
Boost / Ad	
Description	
Start	End
Objective	
Target Audience	
Budget$ / Cost Per Day$	
Landing Page	
Tracking Link	

Text

Demographic

Image

To Do

	Priority	Completed

Editorial Calendar

Month

SUNDAY	MONDAY	TUESDAY	WEDNESDAY	THURSDAY	FRIDAY	SATURDAY

Notes

Acknowledge and Celebrate Your Success

Month:

Total Followers

Post with most engagement (Reposts, Likes, and Comments) on Instagram

---

Post with most clicks

Blog post with most traffic from Instagram

This month, I learned

A record I broke this month

My celebration this month

Next month, I plan to do the same

Next month, I plan to try (new)

Monthly Stats

GOAL:

Total Followers	New Followers	# of Posts	# of Reposts	# of Likes	# of Comments	# of Mentions	# of Clicks	# of Clicks to Website

EMAIL SUBSCRIBERS FROM INSTAGRAM	
ENGAGEMENT	
Post with most reposts	
Post with most likes	
Post with most comments	
Post with most clicks	
INSTAGRAM ADS	

Spend $		Results	

Post Tracker

Instagram Posts	Call to Action	Date	Time	✓

Post Tracker

Instagram MARKETING

Instagram Posts	Call to Action	Date	Time	✓

Video Schedule

Video	Date	Time	✓
#			
#			
#			
#			
#			
#			
#			
#			
#			
#			
#			
#			
#			
#			
#			
#			
#			
#			
#			
#			
#			
#			
#			
#			
#			
#			
#			

Stories Schedule

Use Instagram stories to boost engagement. Post photos in a slideshow or a quick video that will be gone in 24 hours. Perfect for announcements, rants and behind-the-scenes posts.

Stories	Date	Time	✓
#			
#			
#			
#			
#			
#			
#			
#			
#			
#			
#			
#			
#			
#			
#			
#			
#			
#			
#			
#			
#			
#			
#			
#			
#			
#			

Live Tracker

Instagram Live	Date	Time	✓
#			
#			
#			
#			
#			
#			
#			
#			
#			
#			
#			
#			
#			
#			
#			
#			
#			
#			
#			
#			
#			
#			
#			
#			
#			
#			

Product / Service Campaign

Campaign	
Description	
Product / Service / Newsletter / Contest / Giveaway	
Start	End
Objective	
Target Audience	
Budget$ / Cost$ / Return$	
Landing Page	
Tracking Link	
Days and Time	
Winner / Date Notified	

Image

- ☐ Blog Post Announcement
- ☐ Blog Post Follow-up
- ☐ Autoresponder Setup
- ☐ Ad Campaign
  - Budget$
  - Cost$
  - Return$
  - Click Thru Rate
  - CPC (Cost per Click)
- ☐ Conversion Rate
- ☐ Hashtag
- ☐ Coupon Code (if applicable)

Advertising Campaign

Campaign	
Boost / Ad	
Description	
Start	End
Objective	
Target Audience	
Budget$ / Cost Per Day$	
Landing Page	
Tracking Link	

Text

Demographic

Image

To Do

	Priority	Completed

Notes

Month

SUNDAY	MONDAY	TUESDAY	WEDNESDAY	THURSDAY	FRIDAY	SATURDAY

Notes

Acknowledge and Celebrate Your Success

Month:

Total Followers

Post with most engagement (Reposts, Likes, and Comments) on Instagram

---

Post with most clicks

Blog post with most traffic from Instagram

This month, I learned

A record I broke this month

My celebration this month

Next month, I plan to do the same

Next month, I plan to try (new)

Monthly Stats

GOAL:

Total Followers	New Followers	# of Posts	# of Reposts	# of Likes	# of Comments	# of Mentions	# of Clicks	# of Clicks to Website

EMAIL SUBSCRIBERS FROM INSTAGRAM	
ENGAGEMENT	
Post with most reposts	
Post with most likes	
Post with most comments	
Post with most clicks	
INSTAGRAM ADS	

Spend $		Results	

Post Tracker

Instagram Posts	Call to Action	Date	Time	✓

Post Tracker

Instagram Posts	Call to Action	Date	Time	✓

Video Schedule

Video	Date	Time	✓
#			
#			
#			
#			
#			
#			
#			
#			
#			
#			
#			
#			
#			
#			
#			
#			
#			
#			
#			
#			
#			
#			
#			
#			
#			
#			
#			

Stories Schedule

Use Instagram stories to boost engagement. Post photos in a slideshow or a quick video that will be gone in 24 hours. Perfect for announcements, rants and behind-the-scenes posts.

Stories	Date	Time	✓
#			
#			
#			
#			
#			
#			
#			
#			
#			
#			
#			
#			
#			
#			
#			
#			
#			
#			
#			
#			
#			
#			
#			
#			
#			
#			

Live Tracker

Instagram Live	Date	Time	✓
#			
#			
#			
#			
#			
#			
#			
#			
#			
#			
#			
#			
#			
#			
#			
#			
#			
#			
#			
#			
#			
#			
#			
#			
#			
#			

Product / Service Campaign

Campaign	
Description	
Product / Service / Newsletter / Contest / Giveaway	
Start	End
Objective	
Target Audience	
Budget$ / Cost$ / Return$	
Landing Page	
Tracking Link	
Days and Time	
Winner / Date Notified	

Image

- ☐ Blog Post Announcement
- ☐ Blog Post Follow-up
- ☐ Autoresponder Setup
- ☐ Ad Campaign
  - Budget$
  - Cost$
  - Return$
  - Click Thru Rate
  - CPC (Cost per Click)
- ☐ Conversion Rate
- ☐ Hashtag
- ☐ Coupon Code (if applicable)

Advertising Campaign

Campaign	
Boost / Ad	
Description	
Start	End
Objective	
Target Audience	
Budget$ / Cost Per Day$	
Landing Page	
Tracking Link	

Text

Demographic

Image

To Do

	Priority	Completed

Month

SUNDAY	MONDAY	TUESDAY	WEDNESDAY	THURSDAY	FRIDAY	SATURDAY

Notes

Acknowledge and Celebrate Your Success

Month:

Total Followers

Post with most engagement (Reposts, Likes, and Comments) on Instagram

---

Post with most clicks

Blog post with most traffic from Instagram

This month, I learned

A record I broke this month

My celebration this month

Next month, I plan to do the same

Next month, I plan to try (new)

Monthly Stats

GOAL:

Total Followers	New Followers	# of Posts	# of Reposts	# of Likes	# of Comments	# of Mentions	# of Clicks	# of Clicks to Website

EMAIL SUBSCRIBERS FROM INSTAGRAM	

ENGAGEMENT

Post with most reposts	
Post with most likes	
Post with most comments	
Post with most clicks	

INSTAGRAM ADS

Spend $		Results	

Post Tracker

Instagram Posts	Call to Action	Date	Time	✓

Post Tracker

Instagram Posts	Call to Action	Date	Time	✓

Video Schedule

Video	Date	Time	✓
#			
#			
#			
#			
#			
#			
#			
#			
#			
#			
#			
#			
#			
#			
#			
#			
#			
#			
#			
#			
#			
#			
#			
#			
#			
#			
#			

Stories Schedule

Use Instagram stories to boost engagement. Post photos in a slideshow or a quick video that will be gone in 24 hours. Perfect for announcements, rants and behind-the-scenes posts.

Stories	Date	Time	✓
#			
#			
#			
#			
#			
#			
#			
#			
#			
#			
#			
#			
#			
#			
#			
#			
#			
#			
#			
#			
#			
#			
#			
#			
#			
#			

Live Tracker

Instagram Live	Date	Time	✓
#			
#			
#			
#			
#			
#			
#			
#			
#			
#			
#			
#			
#			
#			
#			
#			
#			
#			
#			
#			
#			
#			
#			
#			
#			
#			

Product / Service Campaign

Campaign	
Description	
Product / Service / Newsletter / Contest / Giveaway	
Start	End
Objective	
Target Audience	
Budget$ / Cost$ / Return$	
Landing Page	
Tracking Link	
Days and Time	
Winner / Date Notified	

Image

- ☐ Blog Post Announcement
- ☐ Blog Post Follow-up
- ☐ Autoresponder Setup
- ☐ Ad Campaign
  - Budget$
  - Cost$
  - Return$
  - Click Thru Rate
  - CPC (Cost per Click)
- ☐ Conversion Rate
- ☐ Hashtag
- ☐ Coupon Code (if applicable)

Advertising Campaign

Campaign	
Boost / Ad	
Description	
Start	End
Objective	
Target Audience	
Budget$ / Cost Per Day$	
Landing Page	
Tracking Link	

Text

Demographic

Image

To Do

	Priority	Completed

Notes

Month

SUNDAY	MONDAY	TUESDAY	WEDNESDAY	THURSDAY	FRIDAY	SATURDAY

Notes

Acknowledge and Celebrate Your Success

Month:

Total Followers

Post with most engagement (Reposts, Likes, and Comments) on Instagram

Post with most clicks

Blog post with most traffic from Instagram

This month, I learned

A record I broke this month

My celebration this month

Next month, I plan to do the same

Next month, I plan to try (new)

Monthly Stats

GOAL:

Total Followers	New Followers	# of Posts	# of Reposts	# of Likes	# of Comments	# of Mentions	# of Clicks	# of Clicks to Website

EMAIL SUBSCRIBERS FROM INSTAGRAM	

ENGAGEMENT

Post with most reposts	
Post with most likes	
Post with most comments	
Post with most clicks	

INSTAGRAM ADS

Spend $		Results	

Post Tracker

Instagram Posts	Call to Action	Date	Time	✓

Post Tracker

Instagram Posts	Call to Action	Date	Time	✓

Video Schedule

Video	Date	Time	✓
#			
#			
#			
#			
#			
#			
#			
#			
#			
#			
#			
#			
#			
#			
#			
#			
#			
#			
#			
#			
#			
#			
#			
#			
#			
#			
#			

Stories Schedule

Use Instagram stories to boost engagement. Post photos in a slideshow or a quick video that will be gone in 24 hours. Perfect for announcements, rants and behind-the-scenes posts.

Stories	Date	Time	✓
#			
#			
#			
#			
#			
#			
#			
#			
#			
#			
#			
#			
#			
#			
#			
#			
#			
#			
#			
#			
#			
#			
#			
#			
#			
#			

Live Tracker

Instagram Live	Date	Time	✓
#			
#			
#			
#			
#			
#			
#			
#			
#			
#			
#			
#			
#			
#			
#			
#			
#			
#			
#			
#			
#			
#			
#			
#			
#			
#			

Product / Service Campaign

Campaign	
Description	
Product / Service / Newsletter / Contest / Giveaway	
Start	End
Objective	
Target Audience	
Budget$ / Cost$ / Return$	
Landing Page	
Tracking Link	
Days and Time	
Winner / Date Notified	

Image

- ☐ Blog Post Announcement
- ☐ Blog Post Follow-up
- ☐ Autoresponder Setup
- ☐ Ad Campaign
  - Budget$
  - Cost$
  - Return$
  - Click Thru Rate
  - CPC (Cost per Click)
- ☐ Conversion Rate
- ☐ Hashtag
- ☐ Coupon Code (if applicable)

Advertising Campaign

Campaign	
Boost / Ad	
Description	
Start	End
Objective	
Target Audience	
Budget$ / Cost Per Day$	
Landing Page	
Tracking Link	

Text

Demographic

Imagè

To Do

	Priority	Completed

Notes

Editorial Calendar

Instagram MARKETING

Month

SUNDAY	MONDAY	TUESDAY	WEDNESDAY	THURSDAY	FRIDAY	SATURDAY

Notes

Acknowledge and Celebrate Your Success

Month:

Total Followers

Post with most engagement (Reposts, Likes, and Comments) on Instagram

---

Post with most clicks

Blog post with most traffic from Instagram

This month, I learned

A record I broke this month

My celebration this month

Next month, I plan to do the same

Next month, I plan to try (new)

Monthly Stats

GOAL:

Total Followers	New Followers	# of Posts	# of Reposts	# of Likes	# of Comments	# of Mentions	# of Clicks	# of Clicks to Website

EMAIL SUBSCRIBERS FROM INSTAGRAM	

ENGAGEMENT	
Post with most reposts	
Post with most likes	
Post with most comments	
Post with most clicks	

INSTAGRAM ADS			
Spend $		Results	

Post Tracker

Instagram Posts	Call to Action	Date	Time	✓

Post Tracker

Instagram Posts	Call to Action	Date	Time	✓

Video Schedule

Video	Date	Time	✓
#			
#			
#			
#			
#			
#			
#			
#			
#			
#			
#			
#			
#			
#			
#			
#			
#			
#			
#			
#			
#			
#			
#			
#			
#			
#			
#			

Stories Schedule

Use Instagram stories to boost engagement. Post photos in a slideshow or a quick video that will be gone in 24 hours. Perfect for announcements, rants and behind-the-scenes posts.

Stories	Date	Time	✓
#			
#			
#			
#			
#			
#			
#			
#			
#			
#			
#			
#			
#			
#			
#			
#			
#			
#			
#			
#			
#			
#			
#			
#			
#			
#			

Live Tracker

Instagram Live	Date	Time	✓
#			
#			
#			
#			
#			
#			
#			
#			
#			
#			
#			
#			
#			
#			
#			
#			
#			
#			
#			
#			
#			
#			
#			
#			
#			
#			

Product / Service Campaign

Campaign	
Description	
Product / Service / Newsletter / Contest / Giveaway	
Start	End
Objective	
Target Audience	
Budget$ / Cost$ / Return$	
Landing Page	
Tracking Link	
Days and Time	
Winner / Date Notified	

Image

- ☐ Blog Post Announcement
- ☐ Blog Post Follow-up
- ☐ Autoresponder Setup
- ☐ Ad Campaign
  - Budget$
  - Cost$
  - Return$
  - Click Thru Rate
  - CPC (Cost per Click)
- ☐ Conversion Rate
- ☐ Hashtag
- ☐ Coupon Code (if applicable)

Advertising Campaign

Campaign	
Boost / Ad	
Description	
Start	End
Objective	
Target Audience	
Budget$ / Cost Per Day$	
Landing Page	
Tracking Link	

Text

Demographic

Image

To Do

	Priority	Completed

Month

SUNDAY	MONDAY	TUESDAY	WEDNESDAY	THURSDAY	FRIDAY	SATURDAY

Notes

Acknowledge and Celebrate Your Success

Month:

Total Followers

Post with most engagement (Reposts, Likes, and Comments) on Instagram

Post with most clicks

Blog post with most traffic from Instagram

This month, I learned

A record I broke this month

My celebration this month

Next month, I plan to do the same

Next month, I plan to try (new)

Monthly Stats

GOAL:

Total Followers	New Followers	# of Posts	# of Reposts	# of Likes	# of Comments	# of Mentions	# of Clicks	# of Clicks to Website

EMAIL SUBSCRIBERS FROM INSTAGRAM	
ENGAGEMENT	
Post with most reposts	
Post with most likes	
Post with most comments	
Post with most clicks	
INSTAGRAM ADS	

Spend $		Results	

Post Tracker

Instagram Posts	Call to Action	Date	Time	✓

Post Tracker

Instagram Posts	Call to Action	Date	Time	✓

Video Schedule

Video	Date	Time	✓
#			
#			
#			
#			
#			
#			
#			
#			
#			
#			
#			
#			
#			
#			
#			
#			
#			
#			
#			
#			
#			
#			
#			
#			
#			
#			
#			

Stories Schedule

Use Instagram stories to boost engagement. Post photos in a slideshow or a quick video that will be gone in 24 hours. Perfect for announcements, rants and behind-the-scenes posts.

Stories	Date	Time	✓
#			
#			
#			
#			
#			
#			
#			
#			
#			
#			
#			
#			
#			
#			
#			
#			
#			
#			
#			
#			
#			
#			
#			
#			
#			
#			

Live Tracker

Instagram Live	Date	Time	✓
#			
#			
#			
#			
#			
#			
#			
#			
#			
#			
#			
#			
#			
#			
#			
#			
#			
#			
#			
#			
#			
#			
#			
#			
#			
#			
#			

Product / Service Campaign

Campaign	
Description	
Product / Service / Newsletter / Contest / Giveaway	
Start	End
Objective	
Target Audience	
Budget$ / Cost$ / Return$	
Landing Page	
Tracking Link	
Days and Time	
Winner / Date Notified	

Image

- ☐ Blog Post Announcement
- ☐ Blog Post Follow-up
- ☐ Autoresponder Setup
- ☐ Ad Campaign
  - Budget$
  - Cost$
  - Return$
  - Click Thru Rate
  - CPC (Cost per Click)
- ☐ Conversion Rate
- ☐ Hashtag
- ☐ Coupon Code (if applicable)

Advertising Campaign

Campaign	
Boost / Ad	
Description	
Start	End
Objective	
Target Audience	
Budget$ / Cost Per Day$	
Landing Page	
Tracking Link	

Text	Demographic

	Image

To Do

	Priority	Completed

Notes

Month

SUNDAY	MONDAY	TUESDAY	WEDNESDAY	THURSDAY	FRIDAY	SATURDAY

Notes

Acknowledge and Celebrate Your Success

Month:

Total Followers

Post with most engagement (Reposts, Likes, and Comments) on Instagram

Post with most clicks

Blog post with most traffic from Instagram

This month, I learned

A record I broke this month

My celebration this month

Next month, I plan to do the same

Next month, I plan to try (new)

Monthly Stats

GOAL:

Total Followers	New Followers	# of Posts	# of Reposts	# of Likes	# of Comments	# of Mentions	# of Clicks	# of Clicks to Website

EMAIL SUBSCRIBERS FROM INSTAGRAM	
ENGAGEMENT	
Post with most reposts	
Post with most likes	
Post with most comments	
Post with most clicks	

INSTAGRAM ADS			
Spend $		Results	

Post Tracker

Instagram Posts	Call to Action	Date	Time	✓

Post Tracker

Instagram Posts	Call to Action	Date	Time	✓

Video Schedule

Video	Date	Time	✓
#			
#			
#			
#			
#			
#			
#			
#			
#			
#			
#			
#			
#			
#			
#			
#			
#			
#			
#			
#			
#			
#			
#			
#			
#			
#			
#			
#			

Stories Schedule

Use Instagram stories to boost engagement. Post photos in a slideshow or a quick video that will be gone in 24 hours. Perfect for announcements, rants and behind-the-scenes posts.

Stories	Date	Time	✓
#			
#			
#			
#			
#			
#			
#			
#			
#			
#			
#			
#			
#			
#			
#			
#			
#			
#			
#			
#			
#			
#			
#			
#			
#			
#			

Live Tracker

Instagram Live	Date	Time	✓
#			
#			
#			
#			
#			
#			
#			
#			
#			
#			
#			
#			
#			
#			
#			
#			
#			
#			
#			
#			
#			
#			
#			
#			
#			
#			

Product / Service Campaign

Campaign	
Description	
Product / Service / Newsletter / Contest / Giveaway	
Start	End
Objective	
Target Audience	
Budget$ / Cost$ / Return$	
Landing Page	
Tracking Link	
Days and Time	
Winner / Date Notified	

Image

- ☐ Blog Post Announcement
- ☐ Blog Post Follow-up
- ☐ Autoresponder Setup
- ☐ Ad Campaign
  - Budget$
  - Cost$
  - Return$
  - Click Thru Rate
  - CPC (Cost per Click)
- ☐ Conversion Rate
- ☐ Hashtag
- ☐ Coupon Code (if applicable)

Advertising Campaign

Campaign	
Boost / Ad	
Description	
Start	End
Objective	
Target Audience	
Budget$ / Cost Per Day$	
Landing Page	
Tracking Link	

Text	Demographic

Image

To Do

	Priority	Completed

HOPE YOU ENJOYED USING
YOUR INSTAGRAM WORKBOOK AND PLANNER

GET YOUR FREE WEEKLY INSTAGRAM PLANNER!
http://bit.ly/instagramweekly

PLEASE LEAVE A REVIEW ON AMAZON

BE SURE TO GRAB YOUR COPIES
- Social Media Marketing Workbook -
- Social Media Marketing Planner -
- Google+ Workbook and Planner -
- LinkedIn Workbook and Planner -
- Facebook Workbook and Planner -
- Pinterest Workbook and Planner -
- Twitter Workbook and Planner -

ALSO LOOK OUT FOR
Social Media Marketing: How to Master Engagement in 15 Minutes a Day

Fall in Love with Blogging: From Passion to Plan to Profit

Death of A Website: Don't Make These 7 Killer Website Mistakes

Connect with Dwainia Grey on LinkedIn, Google+, Facebook,
Twitter, Pinterest and Instagram
dwainiagrey.me

Made in the USA
Monee, IL
07 November 2026

67981960R00103